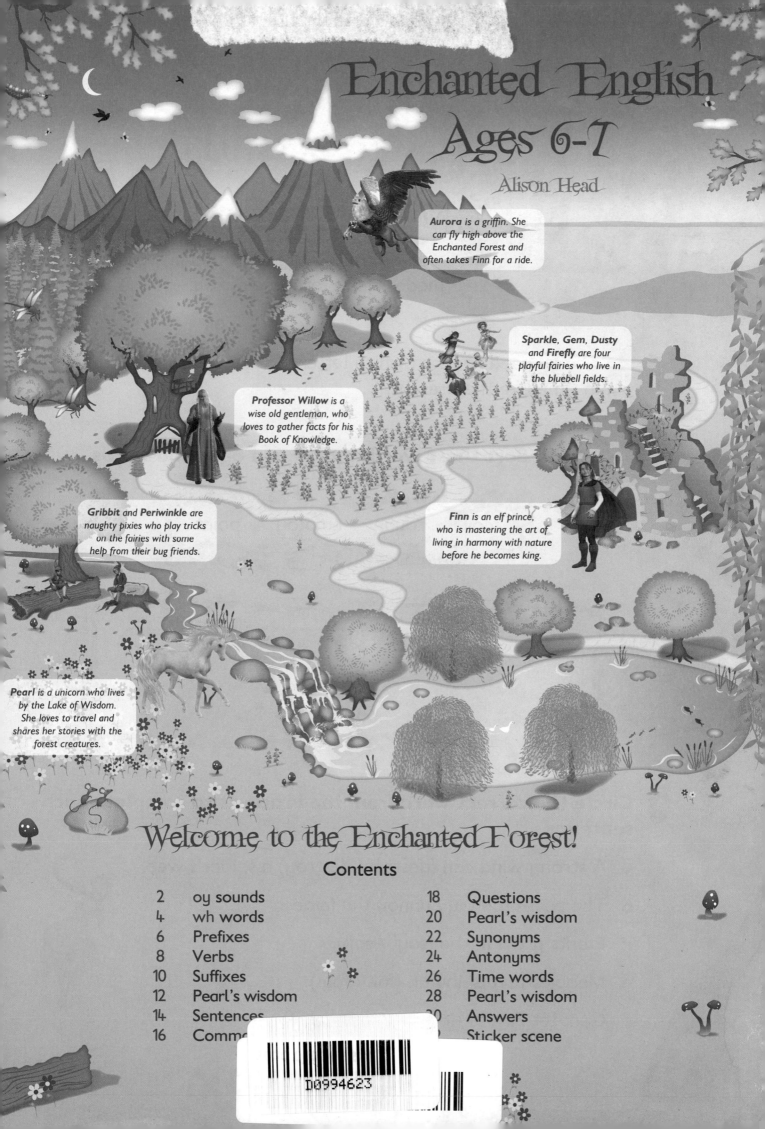

Enchanted English
Ages 6–7
Alison Head

Aurora is a griffin. She can fly high above the Enchanted Forest and often takes Finn for a ride.

Sparkle, **Gem**, **Dusty** and **Firefly** are four playful fairies who live in the bluebell fields.

Professor Willow is a wise old gentleman, who loves to gather facts for his Book of Knowledge.

Gribbit and **Periwinkle** are naughty pixies who play tricks on the fairies with some help from their bug friends.

Finn is an elf prince, who is mastering the art of living in harmony with nature before he becomes king.

Pearl is a unicorn who lives by the Lake of Wisdom. She loves to travel and shares her stories with the forest creatures.

Welcome to the Enchanted Forest!

Contents

2   oy sounds
4   wh words
6   Prefixes
8   Verbs
10   Suffixes
12   Pearl's wisdom
14   Sentences
16   Comm...
18   Questions
20   Pearl's wisdom
22   Synonyms
24   Antonyms
26   Time words
28   Pearl's wisdom
30   Answers
     Sticker scene

oy sounds

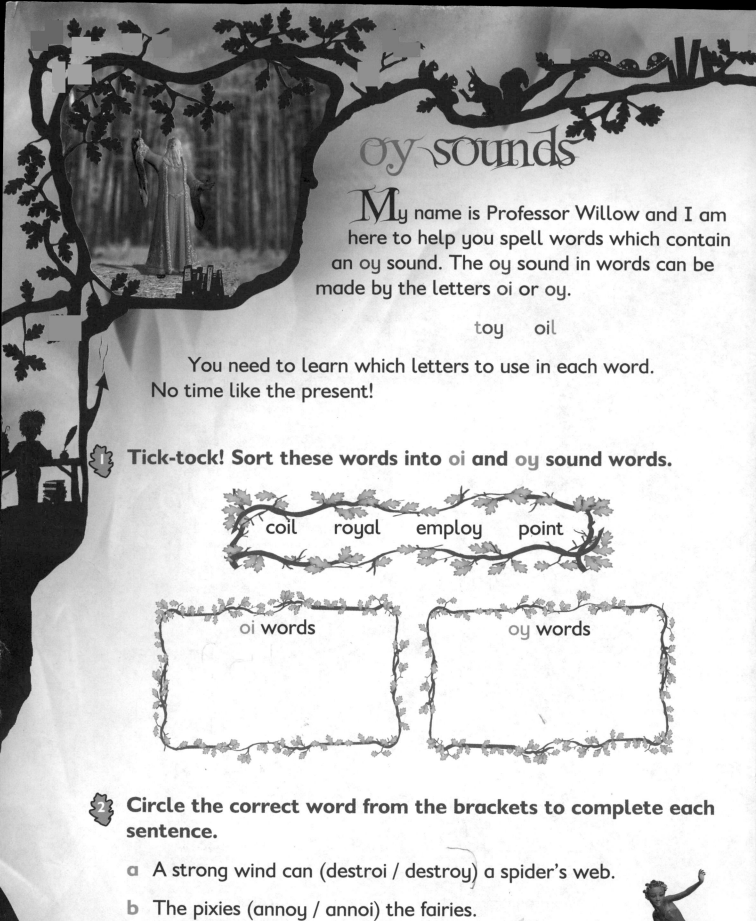

My name is Professor Willow and I am here to help you spell words which contain an oy sound. The oy sound in words can be made by the letters oi or oy.

toy   oil

You need to learn which letters to use in each word. No time like the present!

1 **Tick-tock! Sort these words into oi and oy sound words.**

coil   royal   employ   point

oi words	oy words

2 **Circle the correct word from the brackets to complete each sentence.**

a A strong wind can (destroi / destroy) a spider's web.

b The pixies (annoy / annoi) the fairies.

c Plants grow in the (soyl / soil).

d Magpies love shiny tin (foil / foyl).

e Gem let Firefly (joyn / join) in her game.

3 **Now write sentences using each of these words.**

a **joy** _____

_____

b **boy** _____

_____

c **boil** _____

_____

d **enjoy** _____

_____

Willow's Quest

See if you can find these **oy** sound words in my word search. It is as easy as **A-B-C!**

loyal

appoint

toil

joint

joy

l	b	j	o	i	n	t
o	c	g	t	o	i	l
y	e	d	j	m	h	s
a	p	p	o	i	n	t
l	f	r	y	n	u	i

Find the map at the back of the book and add the sticker of my  Book of Knowledge.

wh words

We are Gribbit and Periwinkle.
We go everywhere together and some letters
are often seen together too! Lots of words
contain the letters wh. The h often makes no
sound, but you must learn when to add it after w!

When will the
squirrel find
some nuts?

1 **Underline the silent h in these wh words.**

a whisper   b whatever   c where

d whirl   e which   f whale

2 **Circle the correctly spelt word from each pongy pair.**

a wat   what

b whose   hoose

c whant   want

d watch   whatch

3 Now find and underline the wh in each squelchy sentence.

a <u>Wh</u>atever Gem is doing, Firefly wants to do too.

b Pearl keeps a diary <u>wh</u>erever she travels.

c Professor Willow loves visitors, <u>wh</u>oever they are.

d <u>Wh</u>enever strangers enter the forest, we scare them away.

e The rabbit twitched its <u>wh</u>iskers, then ran off.

f Finn has a magical <u>wh</u>istle that sounds like a bird singing.

g Fluffy <u>wh</u>ite clouds floated across the sky.

Willow's Quest

Pick a wh word from the box to complete each sentence.

when   what   why   where

a Professor Willow always knows _____ it is going to rain.

b I wonder _____ the fairies do not like the pixies.

c Gribbit showed Periwinkle _____ to find the best acorns.

d _____ has Finn found in his cave?

Add the rabbit and squirrel sticker to the map. Bugalicious!

Prefixes

Flit, flit! We are Dusty and Firefly. Prefixes are groups of letters that can be added to the start of some words to change their meaning. The prefixes un and dis can make some words mean the opposite.

lock   unlock

able   unable

appear   disappear

1 Swirl some fairy dust over these word sums.

a un + tidy = _____

c dis + obey = _____

b dis + able = _____

d un + kind = _____

2 Circle the correct word in each pair of toadstools.

a unfortunate   disfortunate

d disdo   undo

b unhonest   dishonest

e unblock   disblock

c disagree   unagree

3 Wave your wand and write down what each of these words means.

a unhappy

b disagree

c unsure

d dislike

e unclear

f unfriendly

g unchanged

Willow's Quest

Can you change usual to unusual? This cat looks just like cats usually do. See how unusual you can make it look. You could give it wings, or colour it purple!

Add the sticker of the bluebells to the map.

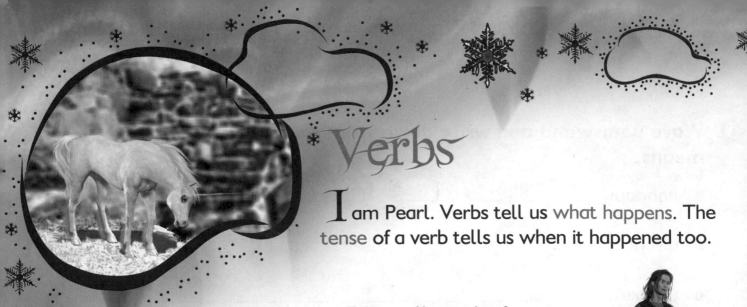

Verbs

I am Pearl. Verbs tell us what happens. The tense of a verb tells us when it happened too.

Finn walks in the forest.
= present tense

Finn walked in the forest.
= past tense

Many past tense verbs end in ed, but some have other endings.

Use the magic within you to underline the past tense verb in each sentence.

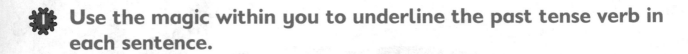

a Pearl visited the Mysterious Mountain.

b Professor Willow worked in his study.

c The fairies flew around the forest.

d The mother robin fed its babies.

e Gribbit fell over a large rock.

f The fox cubs played in the sunshine.

g Finn watched the sunrise.

h Aurora visited Pearl today.

2 Can you circle the past tense verbs?

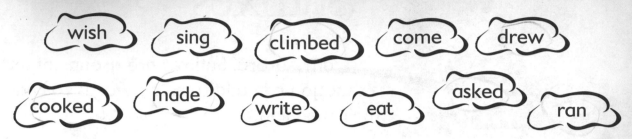

wish   sing   climbed   come   drew

cooked   made   write   eat   asked   ran

3 Underline the correct past tense verb from the brackets to complete each sentence.

a A green frog (jumped / jump) into the Lake of Wisdom.

b Sparkle (worry / worried) when she could not find her wand.

c Aurora (found / find) new treasures for her nest.

d Last week Gribbit and Periwinkle (played / play) a trick on the fairies.

e It (rain / rained) all day yesterday.

Willow's Quest

Now draw lines to match up the pairs of present and past tense verbs. You can do this with a swish of your tail!

a take   watched

b drop   threw

c clean   dropped

d watch   took

e throw   cleaned

Add the unicorns sticker to the map. Swish, swish!

Suffixes

I am Aurora. Suffixes are groups of letters that you can add to some words to change their meaning.

love + ly = lovely

care + ful = careful

If the word ends with a consonant followed by y, you must change the y to i before you add the suffix.

plenty + ful = plentiful

1 **First, underline the suffix in each sentence.**

   a helpful   **b** warmly   **c** powerful

   d joyful   **e** fairly   **f** rapidly

2 **The sky is the limit with suffixes! See if you can complete these word sums.**

   a kind + _____ = kindly

   b play + _____ = playful

   c quick + _____ = quickly

   d colour + _____ = colourful

   e slow + _____ = slowly

   f boast + _____ = boastful

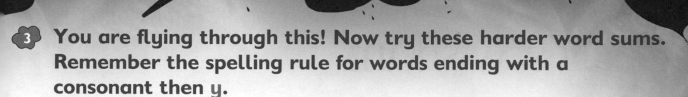

3 You are flying through this! Now try these harder word sums. Remember the spelling rule for words ending with a consonant then **y**.

a beauty + ful = _beautiful_

b pretty + ly = _____

c happy + ly = _____

d lazy + ly = _____

e duty + ful = _____

4 Find and underline a word in each sentence which ends with **ly** or **ful**.

a The sunset tonight was wonderful.

b Gribbit and Periwinkle often behave badly.

c Gem snapped angrily at Gribbit.

d Aurora is graceful when she flies.

e The squirrel scampered swiftly away.

Willow's Quest

Find the words in the box hidden in the curly snail shell. Colour each word a different colour with your favourite crayons.

| loudly | wishful |
| pitiful | busily |

Pop the flock of birds sticker on the map.

Pearl's wisdom

1 **Swish, swish! See if you can unscramble the letters to make three new oy sound words.**

a oilsp _____

b ejnoying _____

c ltyroya _____

d boiedl _____

2 **Write down wh or w to begin each of these words.**

a _____ith

b _____ether

c _____ill

d _____ater

e _____at

3 **Use the magic within you to add un or dis to each word to make the opposites.**

a qualify _____ e harmed _____

b sure _____ f even _____

c pleased _____ g infect _____

d real _____ h do _____

4 **Write these present tense sentences again, in the past tense. Use the past tense verbs in the box to help you.**

worked   crept   drove   stood   flew

a I stand up on the bus.

_____

b Professor Willow works on a new invention.

_____

c Dad drives us to school.

_____

d The mouse creeps past the cat.

_____

e An owl flies through the treetops.

_____

5 **You can do this with a swish of your tail! Look carefully at this list of words. Circle the words you could add the suffixes ly or ful to.**

a red

b calm

c old

d sad

e boast

f dread

g yesterday

h thought

i dead

Add the shells sticker to your map.

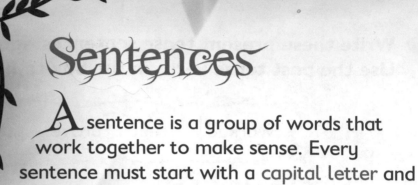

Sentences

A sentence is a group of words that work together to make sense. Every sentence must start with a capital letter and end with a full stop, a question mark or an exclamation mark.

The forest is peaceful.

1 Write each sentence again, with a capital letter and full stop. No time like the present!

a the fairies live amongst the flowers

_____

b finn lives in a lovely palace

_____

2 Match up the pairs of phrases to build three sentences that make sense. Remember to start with a phrase that begins with a capital letter.

Pearl looked at her

Gribbit went to play

Professor Willow

wrote in the Book of Knowledge.

with Periwinkle.

reflection in the Lake of Wisdom.

3 Write your own sentence about each of these topics. If at first you do not succeed, try, try again!

a your friend

_My _____ Mon___ _____

b your home

_M _____

c the weather

_____

d dinosaurs

_Di__ _____ ou _____

e the ocean

_____

Willow's Quest

Let's see how much you remember about sentences. Try to fill in the gaps in this piece of writing.

A sentence is _____

_____. They must begin

with a _____.

They must end with a _____, a question mark

or an exclamation mark.

Add the frog sticker to the map.

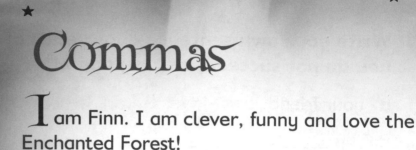

Commas

I am Finn. I am clever, funny and love the Enchanted Forest!

You can use commas to separate the items in a list. Take care though, word warrior, because you must never use a comma before the final and in a list.

In the forest I saw a squirrel, two mice, a hedgehog and a fox.

1 **Can you focus on underlining the final and in these sentences?**

a Pearl has visited the Mysterious Mountains, the Silent Sea and the Creepy Caves.

b Aurora flies Finn to the Lake of Wisdom, the Glade of Yesterday and the Elf Palace.

c The fairies are called Firefly, Gem, Sparkle and Dusty.

d I sleep on a bed made from leaves, twigs and moss.

e Gribbit and Periwinkle are friends with the birds, animals and insects.

f Some of the trees in the forest are the oak, the elm and the beech.

2 Now try these sentences. Put a tick in the lantern beside each sentence that has the commas in the correct place.

a Professor Willow loves letters, words and numbers.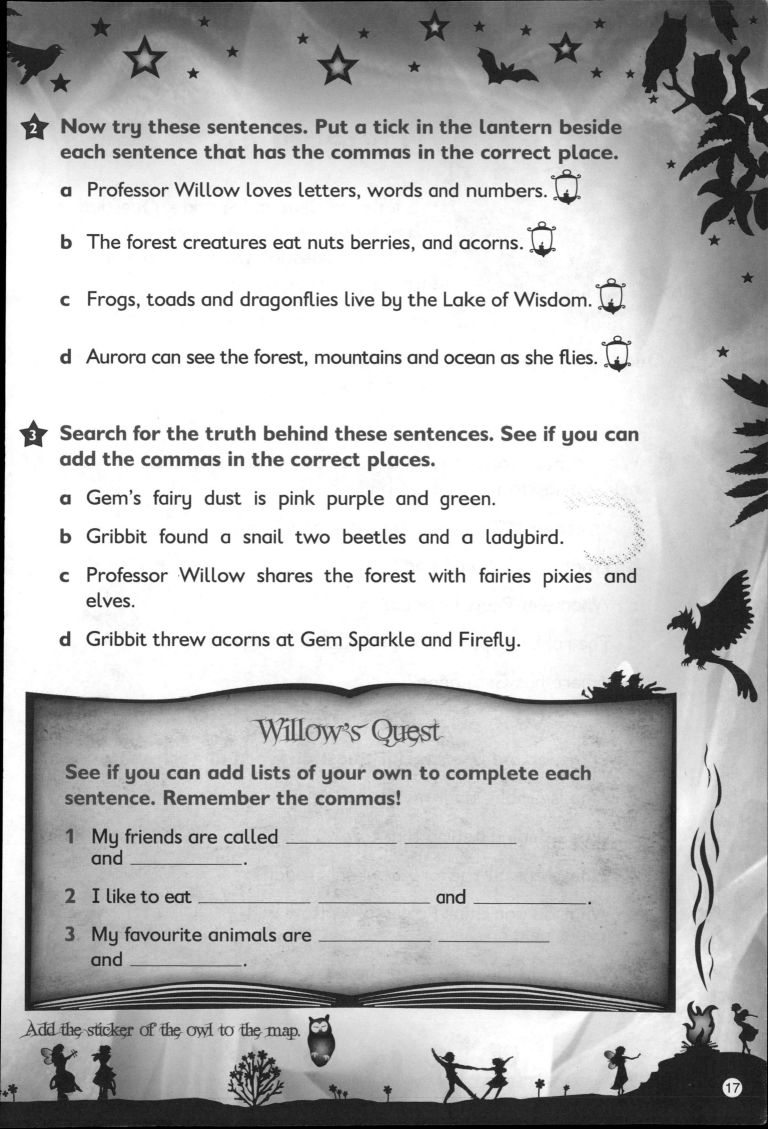

b The forest creatures eat nuts berries, and acorns.

c Frogs, toads and dragonflies live by the Lake of Wisdom.

d Aurora can see the forest, mountains and ocean as she flies.

3 Search for the truth behind these sentences. See if you can add the commas in the correct places.

a Gem's fairy dust is pink purple and green.

b Gribbit found a snail two beetles and a ladybird.

c Professor Willow shares the forest with fairies pixies and elves.

d Gribbit threw acorns at Gem Sparkle and Firefly.

Willow's Quest

See if you can add lists of your own to complete each sentence. Remember the commas!

1 My friends are called _____ _____ and _____.

2 I like to eat _____ _____ and _____.

3 My favourite animals are _____ _____ and _____.

Add the sticker of the owl to the map.

17

Questions

We are Gem and Sparkle. Questions are a great way to ask for information. When we write a question we must end the sentence with a question mark.

Where is Pearl?

Questions often contain special question words like who, what, where, when, how or why.

1 Wave your wand and underline the sentences that ask a question.

  a Professor Willow is by the Lake of Wisdom.

  b What has Gribbit found?

  c When will Pearl be back?

  d The rabbit hopped away through the trees.

  e Where has Gem gone?

2 Now underline the special question word in each sentence.

  a Why is Gribbit angry with the fairies?

  b Who is hiding behind that tree?

  c Where are all the forest animals today?

  d What do you think Professor Willow will invent next?

  e When will Finn return to the palace?

3 Dazzle us with your English skills! Pick the best question word from the box to complete each sentence.

> When   How   Where   Who

a _____ is Pearl talking to?

b _____ is the Lake of Wisdom?

c _____ will the fairies and the pixies make friends?

d _____ does Aurora fly so fast?

4 Think of a good way to end each sentence. Remember to add a question mark!

a Why _____

b Where _____

c When _____

d How _____

e Who _____

Willow's Quest

Read the questions and think about what information each one is asking for. Then write an answer for each.

a What is the name of your school? _____

b How old are you? _____

c Who do you like playing with? _____

Add the dragonflies sticker to the map.

Pearl's wisdom

1 You can do this with a swish of your tail! Write **T** for True or **F** for False next to each of these statements about sentences.

a Sentences are groups of words that work together to make sense. _____

b Many sentences do not start with a capital letter. _____

c All sentences must end with a full stop. _____

d Sentences that ask a question end with a question mark. _____

2 Look at this picture and then use it to complete the sentences. Remember the rules for using commas in lists.

a The three animals that cannot fly are _____

_____ .

b The three creatures flying in the sky are _____

_____ .

c Write your own sentence about what you can see in the picture. Include a list in the sentence. _____

_____

3 **Read this passage and then answer the questions. Look carefully at the question words to help you find the right information.**

Last week, Pearl left the Enchanted Forest because she wanted to visit the Mysterious Mountain. It took her two days to climb to the top of the mountain. At the top, she found a beautiful golden bird. The bird could grant wishes. Pearl wished to be back in her forest glade, playing with Gribbit and Periwinkle.

a When did Pearl leave the Enchanted Forest?

_____

b Why did she leave?

_____

c How long did it take her to climb the mountain?

_____

d What did she find at the top?

_____

e What could the bird do?

_____

f Where did Pearl wish to be?

_____

Use the magic within you to pop the crystals sticker on the map.

Synonyms

Synonym is a tricky word that just means two words that have a similar meaning.

warm   hot

Being able to use synonyms means that you do not have to keep using the same word. That makes your writing much more interesting to read.

① Draw lines to match up these pairs of synonyms. You are a star!

a damp   scary

b cold   new

c sleepy   cool

d frightening   tired

e young   wet

② Now write down a synonym for each of these words.

a big   _____

b small _____

c loud   _____

d fast   _____

e dirty _____

3 You are flying through this! Find and underline one word that is repeated in each sentence.

   a Gem <u>was</u> sad because she was reading a sad story.

   b Pearl wore a beautiful flower in her beautiful mane.

   c Gribbit jogged across the clearing and Periwinkle jogged after him.

   d Professor Willow was happy that Sparkle was happy with her present.

4 Now see if you can write down a synonym for each of the words you underlined.

   a _____   **c** _____

   b _____   **d** _____

Willow's Quest

Use the clues to help you complete the crossword puzzle. The first letter of each word is there to help you.

Across: **1** leap
           3 munch
           5 tug

Down: **2** below
        4 stumble

Crossword grid:
- 1 Across: j u n p
- 2 Down: u n d e r
- 3 Across: e a t
- 4 Down: t r i
- 5 Across/Down: p u l l

Add the hedgehogs sticker to your map.

Antonyms

Words with opposite meanings, like clever and stupid, are called antonyms.

We are clever but the fairies are stupid!

Antonyms are very useful because they help us to compare different things in our writing.

1 **We love to fire our arrows. Draw an arrow between each word and its antonym.**

a big	front
b high	wide
c back	empty
d up	low
e full	down
f narrow	small

2 **Let's get busy! Try writing antonyms for these pongy words.**

a cold _____

b lost _____

c heavy _____

d tidy _____

e on _____

f sad _____

3 Have a go at adding an antonym for the bold words to complete each squelchy sentence.

a Gem was **early** for the party, but Sparkle was _____.

b The forest foxes run **quickly**, but the snails move _____.

c The rabbits play when it is **light**, but the owls come out in the _____.

d Professor Willow sat **inside** and listened to the wind blowing _____.

e Aurora flew **high** over the hills and then swooped _____ over the lake.

Willow's Quest

Here is a picture of Professor Willow and some words that describe him.
Write down antonyms for the words and then use them to draw your own professor.

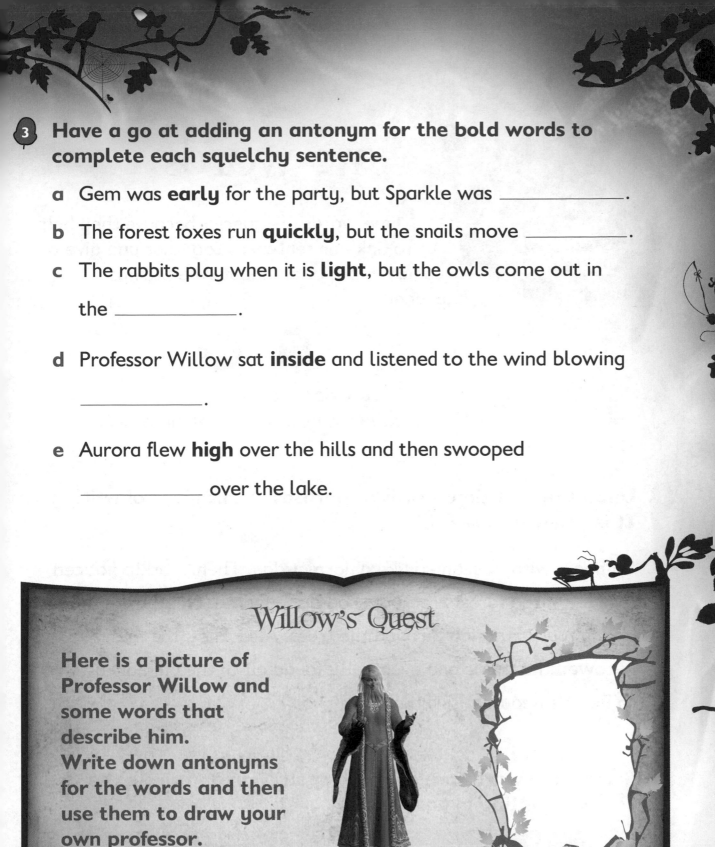

tall _____   thin _____

old _____   clean _____

happy _____

Add the picnic sticker to the map. Bugalicious!

Time words

Time words are special because they help us to link our sentences together and give our readers information about when things happened.

First, Gribbit found an acorn.
After that, Periwinkle found a shiny conker.

1 Underline five time words or phrases in this piece of writing. It is as easy as A-B-C!

To begin with, it seemed like a normal day. Then Sparkle noticed that all of the forest creatures had disappeared. Next, Gem heard lovely music floating through the trees. After that, the fairies followed the music and eventually found all of the animals listening to Pearl's beautiful singing.

2 Some time words are tricky to spell. Can you circle the correct spelling in each pair?

a   furst   first   d   dureing   during

b   finally   finly   e   wyle   while

c   later   layter

3 Pick time words or phrases from the box to complete this passage. If at first you do not succeed, try, try again!

> eventually   At first   During   then   In the end   When

Gribbit found something unusual in the forest. _____ he thought he would keep it, but _____ he decided to show it to Aurora. _____ his journey to her nest, Gribbit got terribly lost but _____ he found it. _____ he arrived, he showed Aurora the mysterious object. They could not decide what it was but agreed that it was very beautiful.

_____ they decided that Aurora should keep it, to add to her collection.

Willow's Quest

Wonderful work! Now unscramble the letters to spell useful time words.

a ngduri   _____

b anwhileme   _____

c neth   _____

d fater   _____

e extn   _____

Pearl's wisdom

1 **You can do this with a swish of your tail! Write a sentence including both words from each pair of synonyms.**

a angry   cross

_____

_____

b crawl   creep

_____

_____

c small   tiny

_____

_____

d shoved   pushed

_____

_____

e slept   dozed

_____

_____

f happy   joyful

_____

_____

2 Circle the word from each group that is an antonym for the bold word.

a **in**   off   (out)   under

b **hard**   (soft)   sticky   spiky

c **dangerous**   risky   (safe)   happy

d **buy**   pay   money   (sell)

e **come**   (go)   arrive   visit

f **awake**   big   (asleep)   travel

3 The sections of this story about one of my travels are all muddled up. Using the bold time words and phrases to help you, see if you can number them 1–5 to put them back in the right order. Just do your best!

a **After** seeing the waterfalls, she sailed across the ocean to a magic island.

b **Eventually**, she returned to the Enchanted Forest to share her stories with her friends.

c **During** the voyage to the island, she met mermaids who told her stories about the sea sprites who ride seahorses beneath the waves.

d The **first** time Pearl left the Enchanted Forest, she travelled to see the Whispering Waterfalls, which whisper secrets to travellers.

e **When** she reached the island she searched for buried treasure.

Find the sticker of the mice fishing for your map.

Answers

Pages 2–3

1

oi words	**oy** words
coil	royal
point	employ

2
a destroy
b annoy
c soil
d foil
e join

3 Sentences will vary.

Willow's Quest

l	b	j	o	i	n	t
o	c	g	t	o	i	l
y	e	d	j	m	h	s
a	p	p	o	i	n	t
l	f	r	y	n	u	i

Pages 4–5

1
a w**h**isper
b w**h**atever
c w**h**ere
d w**h**irl
e w**h**ich
f w**h**ale

2
a what
b whose
c want
d watch

3
a Whatever
b wherever
c whoever
d Whenever
e whiskers
f whistle
g white

Willow's Quest
a when
b why
c where
d What

Pages 6–7

1
a untidy
b disable
c disobey
d unkind

2
a unfortunate
b dishonest
c disagree
d undo
e unblock

3
a not happy
b not agree
c not sure
d not like
e not clear
f not friendly
g not changed

Willow's Quest
Pictures will vary.

Pages 8–9

1
a Pearl <u>visited</u> the Mysterious Mountain.
b Professor Willow <u>worked</u> in his study.
c The fairies <u>flew</u> around the forest.
d The mother robin <u>fed</u> its babies.
e Gribbit <u>fell</u> over a large rock.
f The fox cubs <u>played</u> in the sunshine.
g Finn <u>watched</u> the sunrise.
h Aurora <u>visited</u> Pearl today.

2 The past tense verbs are: climbed, drew, cooked, made, asked and ran.

3
a jumped
b worried
c found
d played
e rained

Willow's Quest
a take — watched
b drop — threw
c clean — dropped
d watch — took
e throw — cleaned

Pages 10–11

1
a help<u>ful</u>
b warm<u>ly</u>
c power<u>ful</u>
d joy<u>ful</u>
e fair<u>ly</u>
f rapid<u>ly</u>

2
a ly
b ful
c ly
d ful
e ly
f ful

3
a beautiful
b prettily
c happily
d lazily
e dutiful

4
a The sunset tonight was <u>wonderful</u>.
b Gribbit and Periwinkle often behave <u>badly</u>.
c Gem snapped <u>angrily</u> at Gribbit.

d Aurora is <u>graceful</u> when she flies.
e The squirrel scampered <u>swiftly</u> away.

Willow's Quest

Pages 12–13

1
a spoil
b enjoying
c royalty
d boiled

2
a with
b whether
c will
d water
e what

3
a disqualify
b unsure
c displeased
d unreal
e unharmed
f uneven
g disinfect
h undo

4
a I stood up on the bus.
b Professor Willow worked on a new invention.
c Dad drove us to school.
d The mouse crept past the cat.
e An owl flew through the treetops.

5 You could add a suffix to words b, d, e, f, h and i.

Pages 14–15

1
a The fairies live amongst the flowers.
b Finn lives in a lovely palace.

2 Pearl looked at her reflection in the Lake of Wisdom.
Gribbit went to play with Periwinkle.
Professor Willow wrote in the Book of Knowledge.

3 Sentences will vary.

Willow's Quest
A sentence is a group of words that work together to make sense. They must begin with a capital letter. They must end with a full stop, a question mark or an exclamation mark.

Pages 16–17

1 a Pearl has visited the Mysterious Mountains, the Silent Sea <u>and</u> the Creepy Caves.
   b Aurora flies Finn to the Lake of Wisdom, the Glade of Yesterday <u>and</u> the Elf Palace.
   c The fairies are called Firefly, Gem, Sparkle <u>and</u> Dusty.
   d I sleep on a bed made from leaves, twigs <u>and</u> moss.
   e Gribbit and Periwinkle are friends with the birds, animals <u>and</u> insects.
   f Some of the trees in the forest are the oak, the elm <u>and</u> the beech.
2 The correct sentences are: a, c and d.
3 a Gem's fairy dust is pink, purple <u>and</u> green.
   b Gribbit found a snail, two beetles and a ladybird.
   c Professor Willow shares the forest with fairies, pixies and elves.
   d Gribbit threw acorns at Gem, Sparkle and Firefly.

Willow's Quest
Answers will vary.

Pages 18–19

1 The questions are: b, c and e.
2 a <u>Why</u> is Gribbit angry with the fairies?
   b <u>Who</u> is hiding behind that tree?
   c <u>Where</u> are all the forest animals today?
   d <u>What</u> do you think Professor Willow will invent next?
   e <u>When</u> will Finn return to the palace?
3 a Who
   b Where
   c When
   d How
4 Answers will vary.

Willow's Quest
Answers will vary.

Pages 20–21

1 a T
   b F
   c F
   d T
2 a The three animals that cannot fly are a rabbit, a hedgehog and a fox.
   b Flying in the sky are two bees, a bird and a butterfly.
   c Answers will vary.
3 a Pearl left the Enchanted Forest last week.
   b She left because she wanted to visit the Mysterious Mountain.
   c It took her two days to climb the mountain.
   d At the top she found a beautiful golden bird.

e The bird could grant wishes.
f Pearl wished to be back in her forest glade.

Pages 22–23

1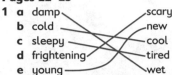
   a damp
   b cold
   c sleepy
   d frightening
   e young
   scary
   new
   cool
   tired
   wet
2 Answers will vary, but might include:
   a huge
   b tiny
   c noisy
   d quick
   e messy
3 a Gem was <u>sad</u> because she was reading a <u>sad</u> story.
   b Pearl wore a <u>beautiful</u> flower in her <u>beautiful</u> mane.
   c Gribbit <u>jogged</u> across the clearing and Periwinkle <u>jogged</u> after him.
   d Professor Willow was <u>happy</u> that Sparkle was <u>happy</u> with her present.
4 Answers will vary, but might include:
   a unhappy
   b pretty
   c ran
   d delighted

Willow's Quest

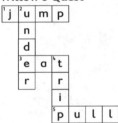

Pages 24–25

1 a big
   b high
   c back
   d up
   e full
   f narrow
   front
   wide
   empty
   low
   down
   small
2 Answers will vary, but might include:
   a hot
   b found
   c light
   d untidy
   e off
   f happy
3 a Gem was **early** for the party, but Sparkle was **late**.
   b The forest foxes run **quickly**, but the snails move **slowly**.
   c The rabbits play when it is **light**, but the owls come out in the **dark**.
   d Professor Willow sat **inside** and listened to the wind blowing **outside**.
   e Aurora flew **high** over the hills and then swooped **low** over the lake.

Willow's Quest
Pictures will vary, but words might include: short, young, unhappy, fat and dirty.

Pages 26–27

1 <u>To begin with</u>, it seemed like a normal day. <u>Then</u> Sparkle noticed that all of the forest creatures had disappeared. <u>Next</u>, Gem heard lovely music floating through the trees. <u>After that</u>, the fairies followed the music and <u>eventually</u> found all of the animals listening to Pearl's beautiful singing.
2 a first
   b finally
   c later
   d during
   e while
3 Gribbit found something unusual in the forest. **At first** he thought he would keep it, but **then** he decided to show it to Aurora. **During** his journey to her nest, Gribbit got terribly lost but **eventually** he found it. **When** he arrived, he showed Aurora the mysterious object. They could not decide what is was but agreed that it was very beautiful. **In the end** they decided that Aurora should keep it, to add to her collection.

Willow's Quest
a during
b meanwhile
c then
d after
e next

Pages 28–29

1 Sentences will vary.
2 a out
   b soft
   c safe
   d sell
   e go
   f asleep
3 The correct order is:
   1 The **first** time Pearl left the Enchanted Forest, she travelled to see the Whispering Waterfalls, which whisper secrets to travellers.
   2 **After** seeing the waterfalls, she sailed across the ocean to a magic island.
   3 **During** the voyage to the island, she met mermaids who told her stories about the sea sprites who ride seahorses beneath the waves.
   4 **When** she reached the island she searched for buried treasure.
   5 **Eventually**, she returned to the Enchanted Forest to share her stories with her friends.

Welcome to the Enchanted Forest...

Wonderful work!